Melbourne
Journal

Alan Loney

Alan Loney is a poet, a handpress printer, and a publisher. His first book of poems was published in 1971, and he has published the poetry of others since 1975. Recent books include *The Books to Come* (Cuneiform 2010), *Bruno Leti: Paintings* (Macmillan 2011), and *The Printing of a Masterpiece* (Black Pepper 2008), and a novella *Anne of the Iron Door* (Black Pepper 2011). Most recent poetry is *conStellations* (Work & Tumble 2015) and an essay, *Death of the reader* (Mindmade Books, Los Angeles 2016). He was winner of the Poetry prize in the 2016 Victorian Premier's Literary Awards with *Crankhandle* (Cordite 2015), received the Janet Frame Literary Trust Award for a life's achievement in poetry in 2011, and was Literary Fellow at the University of Auckland in 1992. He was founder and co-Director of the Holloway Press at the University of Auckland, 1994-1998. He has recently retired from printing at Electio Editions (2004-2015), and is publisher of Verso, a magazine for the Book as a Work of Art. He lives with his partner, Miriam Morris, in Melbourne, Australia.

Alan Loney
Melbourne Journal
Journal
Notebooks 1998–2003

U W
A P
Poetry

First published in 2016 by
UWA Publishing
Crawley, Western Australia 6009
www.uwap.uwa.edu.au

UWAP is an imprint of UWA Publishing
a division of The University of Western Australia

THE UNIVERSITY OF
WESTERN
AUSTRALIA

National Library of Australia
Cataloguing-in-Publication entry:
Loney, Alan, 1940– author.
Melbourne journal : notebooks 1998-2003 / Alan Loney.
ISBN: 9781742589114 (paperback)
Australian poetry—21st century.
Melbourne (Vic.)—Poetry.
A821.3

Designed by Becky Chilcott, Chil3
Typeset in Lyon Text by Lasertype
Printed by Lightning Source

uwapublishing

My earlier notebooks were published under the title *Sidetracks: Notebooks 1976-1991* (Auckland University Press 1998). *Melbourne Journal* continues this process, beginning with my first move to Australia in October 1998. The Notebooks after *Melbourne Journal*, *Crankhandle*, is published by Cordite Books 2015, and won the Victorian Premier's Literary Award for Poetry, 2016. I wish to record here my abiding gratitude to Kris Hemensley for his sharp reading of the text, and to Roger Horrocks, whose gift of a manuscript selection from his own notebooks many years ago still informs and delights me.

Alan Loney
Melbourne
2016

October 1998 – May 1999

Tell me what is happening on earth.
Joseph Joubert, 1797

nothing's familiar. What shall I say
to her. Not a thing
he has ever done has prepared him

Might even poetry be abandoned, that
had never talked to anyone

This morning, he will practise
self esteem

-

what is the journey now imbark't
My necessaries are not around me

Nor are the colours intimate, as if
each one were mixed with grey

Something was supposed to happen
Something was not supposed to happen

And a virtual office, where the demons
have come to roost, as an attachment

-

all my writing life I have regarded poetry as heightened language, in
every way. I want the writing to be technically sound—no, better than
that, I want it technically brilliant whatever one's imperfections. Of
course we get labelled 'clever', as if there is nothing else happening on the
page. And decorum, always

-

(at Daylesford)

/ can you hear the quiet

/ can you see the dark

-

a short stout man walks
into the sea, looks to the sky
a moment, crosses himself
twice, wades into deeper water,
looks up again, crosses himself
again, and dives, his arms
in two great arcs from
his waist, out to his sides
over his head, into
the waves

-

every thing makes the same claim upon him

or, how to scout ahead
of the avant garde

-

writing as a form or mode of waiting

waiting as a mode or form of writing

-

two middle-aged women in dark suits
sit & talk on a bench. A middle-aged man,
well-dressed but without his jacket (how
one assumes he has one!) greets the women,
who greet him. He takes from his pocket
and gives to one of the women a large
roll of banknotes. She looks at it, turns it
over and over in her hands for a moment,
then gives it to the woman beside her, who
does exactly the same with it, then gives it
to the man, who pockets it, and walks off

-

what a supremely *oral* culture we are

-

about poetic form — Foucault's remark on the calligramme — "never
speaks and represents at the same moment" (this from Michel Foucault,
This is not a pipe, trans James Harkness, Univ. of California Press 1983).
When one reads, the shape of the poem, its outer form, disappears. Is
this why, in this indeterminacy, why the formal experiment of twentieth
century poetry (from Gertrude Stein, Dada, Surrealism etc onwards) has
failed in wide social terms? It's not that the experiment didn't work—it
did, does, magnificently—but in terms of mass culture, the form/content
split has widened. It wants presentation merely, and then takes it for the
real. It wants the persona to be the person, the image to be the thing. To
make matters more difficult for writing, the computer permits conserva-
tive writing to become radically shaped, and truly radical work to be laid
out (ouch! "laid out"— cold?) as 'prose'

-

fishing-boat names at Geelong — "Lisa-Jean"

"Mildred Rose"

-

what is the question I want to solve by my current reading? I am struck by the *personal* nature of writings by Sven Birkerts, James J. O'Donnell, Ivan Illich and Barry Sanders. Their inquiries are not merely academic, nor are they intended to be rhetorically or commercially persuasive. Their subject matter is both the substance, the matter, of the book, and the subject that is themselves. Most others I know who have read avidly from an early age—and I did not—typically have fiction as their primary reading or as their most engaging reading experience. I wonder if reading novels is a process most removed from the sort of reading that we actually do in the electronic medium. The *ideal* novel reader (and I might read just one or two in a year) presumably does not take their eyes off the book until the last page is turned. But to read in the electronic medium is to continually make extra-textual and conscious choices about where to click next. For Birkerts et al there are personal issues around reading as a social practice in the wider community based on their own personal attachment to the specifics of their readerly experience. But, in the absence of identification with their issues, what is *my* question, and how will it come to be formulated?

-

why I write with the dictionaries open on the desk—Shorter Oxford 1959, Skeats's Etymological 1963—is to scan all the possible meanings of a word, especially those outside my original intentions, or what I thought I meant—and not just words I don't know, but also words I do or sort of know—for those meanings, at some level and in some measure, will nevertheless echo or resonate differently in the reading by others

-

"the balance may include unclear funds"

-

have just seen that *fragmenta nova* is the new work, here, in Melbourne. So much of what one knows follows after what's done. It keeps giving the slip to truly viable intentions proposed to exist before composition (first I do my think, then I write it) tho I don't doubt at all those realities of intent. . .

-

Emily Dickinson : 'After great pain, a formal feeling comes'

Mary Oliver : 'After a cruel childhood, one must reinvent oneself. Then reimagine the world.'

-

how little, finally, one makes, of everything

-

why is it, tho not always, when one unexpectedly drops something, that one of the immediate & instinctive things one does is to pull the hands *away* from the article, rather than towards it for retrieval before it hits the ground?

-

each day I come to Browns Café, at Albert Park, I look for a thin book to bring with me. Today's is Blanchot's *The Madness of the Day* (*La Folie du Jour*, trans Lydia Davis, Station Hill 1981). On opening : 'Reading was a great weariness for me. . . ', and this so characterises much of my own reading experience. Most of it is just hard slog, and from which I give up more easily these days. The complementary question to 'How will I revitalise my writing?' is therefore 'How can my reading experience be revitalised?'

-

the frequency with which I look up from reading or writing
to see someone go out of the café, that I did not see
or even sense going in

-

across the table, here in the State Library of Victoria, is a man about my age addressing a series of volumes once known as The Blue Books — tho now bound in a brownish cloth — from which he is fastidiously noting wheat yields in Victoria, county by county, at the turn of the century.

I am, for the first time, examining the books (some) and (some) prospectuses of the late Alec Bolton's Brindabella Press: looking at pictures, reading poems, checking out the technical qualities of printing & binding.

What do you have if these two activities are taken together? Wheat yields. The shimmer of pure poetry. Ears for song?

-

re Illich & Sanders — check out their notion of the *pre-alphabetic bard* beside the Language Poets. How might a post-alphabetic bard retrieve pre-alphabetic process? Is it possible? The pre-Homeric poet relied on memory, not of the succession of words in the poem, but of the story as a whole, and of the technics of telling (whether the remaining syllables left in a line would permit 'wise Athene' or 'grey-eyed Athene' etc

-

I find myself to be of such an intense
emotional fragility

-

Illich & Sanders : "The water of memory turns into the fluency of
a writer and a reader."

and this from the proto-poet himself (whose lyre was passed back to Apollo)—Orpheus :
... give me at once cold water
flowing forth from the Lake of Memory
(trans Kathleen Freeman)

-

to what extent can one have access to deep cultural information without reading? Or, what access does the culture already provide to deep cultural information outside of reading?

-

Indeterminacy Principle : one cannot read and overhear the conversation
at the next table at the same time

-

HAMBURGERS INCOGNITO

-

a row of three generations of women
holding hands, all smiles
walking past the café

(tho 'past the café' is less
of their process as of
mine, sitting here,
looking,

voyeur!

-

is it possible, that this place, not
'the land of my birth'
is where I might truly
come to be

'at home'

-

(a graph)

each

one

of

us

an

infinitesimal

flare

in

the

inconceivable

fire

of

creation

-

if I am, as Hugh of St Victor says, to learn, bit by bit,
to leave one's native soil, then that native soil
is not simply the country or the valley
of one's birth, but also the entire range of
assumptions and values by which
one has previously lived   'bit by bit'

-

reading between the lines as being open to the white
page as a mirror to the self

into the light   =   into the page

-

how might those others write of the writer writing them?

-

dream fragment—

photograph of a missing child wearing adult's clothing

-

woke up with these words : "the pail is the content"

pail : vessel or container for carrying liquids
pale : boundary, pointed piece of wood for fence, civilised behaviour, those under the rule of another, ashen, whitish

the options—the body as vessel, with its limits as the content of one's work, one's life; the liquid as the body's water content; the horizon, sea's or any rim as pail's rim, all of it, as the total content of one's attention; that the body and its context are the same, and that's the content and to be content with that; that the rule of law is the limit of one's actions, and there is no such place as 'beyond the pale'

-

a 'body of knowledge' cannot be made visible. There is only the occasional irruption of something into a present discourse. These irruptions or appearances or inventions tend to imply a pool of data which, by memory, we can access at will. But we have no means of doing something like print out everything we know

-

much interested in Illich's idea that Hugh of St Victor might quote from classical sources to 'dis-embed' the sentiment from this or that author, in order to testify to 'untouchable tradition'

-

'overload comes of
too much of the same
kind of
information'

-

what will come of this pain. It is not
as if one just has it, and then
one has something else. Yet

it seems I have always
had it.

Can one decide to
continue to have it (not
as a coat one can wear
or not, but as the skin

one finally acknowledges
one has no choice but to keep
living in

-

a story, say, of one who wished to die
and to do so by flying into a distance
and actually disappearing

-

listen, as it is easy to do in this suburban village, with its long established
Greek and Italian populations, to the conversations of those whose lan-
guage you don't understand. I can't tell where the words end, where the
sentences end, where the subject changes. What I hear is more or less a
continuum of sound interrupted or interspersed with pauses, elongated
vowels, apparent repetitions. Given too that in most languages there are
sounds which writing does not mimic in expectable ways, it is impossible
to write down the noises one thought one heard so the original speaker
would recognise anything they had said, or even recognise it as language
at all

-

alongside Birkerts, place Jerome McGann. Birkerts seems not only not
to know contemporary poetry, but not to be too aware of current textual
theory or editorial theory either. His view of the book as *closure* is almost
naïve

-

learning to find that discreet distance
from a group of birds
so as not to disturb their activity
but to watch them clearly

-

the spectre of 'linear narrative' that hypertext is supposed to supersede is just that, a spectre, a ghostly pretence. While hypertext permits works to be created containing multiple narratives, that's what they are, each one a set narrative beside a multiplicity of other set narratives. 'Closure' does not mean 'one specific text and not another'. Multiple narratives operate a bit like probability theory—all the possibilities are of equal value until one of them is chosen. And that chosen text can be either open or closed. The poetry of open form was developed in order to mimic an openness of nature or consciousness or the creative spirit in its innermost workings. It allowed an ambiguity at the heart of being and of language to be present in the poem as part of the poem's content.

It's curious that most commentators on the so-called 'interface' between the screen and the page equate 'reading books' with 'reading novels'. Poetry is nowhere to be seen. Even this 'interface' is a phoney one, because page and screen have no means of interacting. But the history of twentieth century poetry and book-making are elided, effaced from the discussion, as if they simply had not taken place. Also elided is the huge range of printed matter that is *not* covered by the term 'novel', and which actually constitutes our daily and highly hypertextual engagement with texts. We read a huge number of small texts every day—looking at one's watch, checking the calendar, referring to a diary, reading mail, paying bills, flicking thru magazines, checking street signs, clothes labels, menus, notice boards, credit cards, tram tickets, taxi chits—whatever life we have, it usually entails a considerable number of reading acts that we barely register *as* acts of reading thruout any given day.

The novel is thus clearly a red herring as *the* model for what humans do when they read. Reading a novel is one reading act among others, and it does not describe a daily practice of reading. This practice does not have the page or the screen or any other text-bearing object as its centre: that centre is the person doing the reading

-

note the sheer variety of the physical products of print technology as against the homogenising screen

-

the *anxiety* behind these endless predictions of the technological future. I don't argue against the technology or the computer, nor diminish the role they play in my life, but I do tire of those with money to gain dangling their crystal balls (!) in front of us

-

what's the name of the activity that moves from page to screen and back again, this shuttling back & forth from one modality to another?

-

summer day, dark with rain cloud,
air dampening, the light dulling
the chrome of the cars

the ubiquity of sparrows

the small, almost invisible
things she does for him

-

8.15 am, at the beach, deserted but for an occasional runner, another walking a dog, and I'm sitting on the sand at water's edge. At Port Melbourne two white passenger ships are docked, almost too white to look at in the morning sun. Around me, a few gulls, and out over water a pair of pelicans fly west to east. Beyond South Melbourne pier, a hot-air balloon in the distance, and a cargo ship eases into the harbour. Now and then a small plane and a helicopter pick out paths in the air, and a lone swimmer rounds a yellow marker of some purpose and heads back toward the aforementioned pier

-

three times in my life I vowed I'd never print again. For 25 years and three presses, the smell of printing ink, the sound of it as the rollers pass over metal type, the cool (not wet) touch of damped handmade or mouldmade paper, have absorbed most of my creative and intellectual energy. Now, it's time for me to write—it was always that the more I printed the less I wrote—tho the book, nevertheless, remains an issue

-

I wonder if I enjoy being alone, and more than I have ever admitted. I have spent so much time by myself in recent years that it must have answered some kind of need, or even preference

-

between them, a coffee each and one croissant. She uses a knife to secure the small pieces she takes. He abruptly reaches over, picks up the croissant, takes a large bite from it, dumps the remainder back on the plate, and returns to his newspaper

-

PLEASE BLUSH
AFTER USING

-

Birkerts : 'The formerly stable system—the axis with writer at one end, editor, publisher, and bookseller in the middle, and reader at the other end—is slowly being bent into a pretzel.'

But that 'system' was *never* stable, neither when texts were transmitted by scribes and copyists, nor at the beginning of printing. Compare Shakespeare's First Folio with the Quartos and the Quartos with each other. The instability of textual transmission has always been 'pretzelian'

-

Wittgenstein : 'The horrors of hell can be experienced in a single day: that's plenty of time.'

and '...in the absence of art, the object is just a fragment of nature like any other.'

-

what if, in Bridport Street
of a fine day & people doing
all the usual things at

10.04 am, and without prior
warning

all heaven were to break loose

-

'When flashing, stop
for pedestrians'

-

they were both so skinny
they feared their rib-cages
might interlock

-

getting into the car, a woman in a very short skirt puts one foot inside
the cab, keeping her right foot on the ground before sitting down, then
swings her right foot into the car. Another woman in a trouser suit opens
the door, stands facing at right angle to the car, sits down with knees
together, then swivels both legs round and into the vehicle

-

what on earth
am I on earth for

-

coming into the world
there's no point of no return

-

my senses of being poetically marginalised are deeply ingrained in my
social marginalisation—how I have never been able to survive in any nor-
mal fashion, or be a full member of the social body, or belong to a group,
even if that group was the avant garde in New Zealand poetry

-

it is hard to think clearly about emotional matters when the writer in one takes over at the drop of the first word

-

how to rethink it all, 'make it new', *in writing*, when writing is one of the oldest *habits* I have

-

last morning at Browns for foreseeable future. The money will run out in two weeks. Getting thinner all the time. Email from Max Gimblett tells me I am obviously stripping to whatever is essential—just me & god, is how he puts it. 'Even so, we need to be kind enough to ourselves to provide food and shelter . . .'

-

lying awake around 3 am, I 'remembered' a line from Wittgenstein : 'Poetry can pierce us', and thought, *all* poetry? and wished he had written with greater, and his usual, precision. Later, around 10 am, I opened *Zettel* to find : 'A poet's words can pierce us.' Precision found

-

I am writing a kind of swan-song

-

for a few moments, a woman
at one table looks, with clear curiosity
at a woman at another table.

Her face is alive, a half-smile
'playing', as it's said, about
her mouth. Then quickly

her expression changes. She looks
away toward the footpath,
the liveliness momently

gone from her. What can
one say about it. Nothing can be
implied of her thought or

feeling, tho any guess could
turn out to be correct. In any
case, one isn't going to accost her

and ask her to give an account
of matters

-

at Daylesford—

dozens of cockatoos, as if the gum-tree
sprouted birds instead of flowers

the noise is everywhere, but unlike
city or traffic sound's continuous
drone—it's particular,
a concatenation of
specifics

Watch it, she says, you'll end up
writing ballads from the bush!

-

paid for air-ticket back to New Zealand.

In Caffe Galileo in Clarendon Street, the guitar music is quiet and complex, the coffee is as ever splendid. But where, Galileo, is the starry messenger—your telescope, *sidereus nuncius*—who will tell me what to do next. Am I an artist, or is this a fantasy designed to cover for life-long socio-economic ineptitude? I have made no provision whatever for my later life

-

but the woman there tells me I have
no accent, and nor does she, a
Melburnian who lived in Europe
a few years. That's it then—
unidentifiable by sound

New Zealand
May 1999 – May 2001

Grief keeps watch.
Maurice Blanchot

aventur und kunst (Gutenberg, or so they say

-

he comes out of sleep.
The curtain makes no record
of his movement.
                    He will
cover his small ground
with 'stony rubbish'.

She is drawing. She is
telling the story of the
drawing as she does it.
'It's raining' she says,

and he looks out to see
if it really is.
                    She goes
back to sleep

-

even the birdsong's not
familiar. Cutting
flowerheads I think
how one locale merges
with another in the words
'the language in the air'
he sd, counting the coins
in his open hand

Each attraction distracts

tho all's there
for dear memoir. The new

diet has altered the shape
feel, smell of his
body. Leave it

behind, the native soil
and all those dreams
gifts, pains you ever
lived by

'bit by bit'

-

the tree out my window
has said nothing, repeatedly
all morning
                white paper
                white desk
                white lamp
                white walls
                white lies

-

the dead do not
lie still

the dead lie to you
all the time

-

reductio

strip him down, see, finally
if there's anything worth keeping
His dignity first, that sad
'posture of the body', and the rest
is easy. Cut away his beliefs, values
flay him where his joy resides

Slowly leach all warmth & reassurance
from the room. Tell him
you are waiting for his pennies
to drop, knowing he has no coin
but what you give him

and you nearly have it : a skeleton
that weeps

Go on, why don't you
flick the thigh-bone out
and finish him off

-

he brought home the music, not to his taste, but to his opportunity, which
formed my taste. No song written without its measure of violence, rage,
tenderness, tears. The focus on the dark circle that sang to him has never
left him. While song held him in thrall, songs did not. He did not care for
the words, yet a few phrases, o rose marie, remained, I'm always dream-
ing of you. One can love that sort of noise as one can love the calligraphy
of a language one cannot read. Am I that man, who could no longer
remember words or tunes of the songs he used to sing, but who would, on
request, open his mouth and emit one long high note until his breath gave
out, returning our silence to us. A figure I repeat, like the notes I hum in
the kitchen, or the picture I have of what the world at its best might give
me, for my pains

-

in the privacy of
this unspeakably public act
of betrayal
       the writing pen is
literally, yours, how it fits
my hand
       in a soft wariness
on the page

where is everything else
that is the case

-

out of the dream they come
    the shapes   the letters   the colours
their kindness   their brutal truth
    that keep you quiet
       in your endless pamphleteering

in the glass room   *omphalos*
  unravelled navel   centre of earth
  embossed shield   *amphora*
      wine jar   cinerary urn

everything tells you everything

-

I still love a phrase from Jung, and I can't recall its provenance, but which
has as it were followed me around for about thirty years : 'a constellation
of affective signs' : it too, therefore, being of that very constellation

-

en route : why wait for travelling to be thus en route? It was ever in process, not ceased or stoppable, no stepping off point, no disembarkation. How did we imagine we could set foot, or so interrupt the long or short passage of our dying to be somewhere else other than dead

-

dear heart, how I took myself, from you

-

today's beginning. Its panorama makes this demand, this excessive demand, upon you : you have been looking and listening all your life, you are glutted with its sights and sounds pounding into you without restraint or let-up, and it says to you : here! listen! look again!

-

flout the conventions all you like
they will pop up like morning glories
again tomorrow   and you will
love them in the bed of your
transgressions, your false dreams
your clumsiness when delicate caresses
are called for, your gauche flirtations
when unmistakable intentions are
demanded   they will tell you
'Do it like this
                    and this
and this
          as of old'

-

alienation in one's 'own country' —

as if one had been
deported
to a place
from which one never came

from a place at which
one had never arrived

-

for a brief moment in the café he became suddenly aware of all the talking, or rather the noise of all the talking, from the other tables. For a moment it filled his total attention, hearing it as a wall of sound in which not one articulated syllable could be distinguished, not one sign to which he could attach any kind of meaning, and he felt, in the midst of that sound, or perhaps as part of or even creator of that sound, and for that brief moment, utterly happy

-

did I begin to write
so to be like him

so to be
unlike myself

-

as if to write were to ob-
literate everything you knew

-

I am haunted by a book I cannot read

I am haunted by a book I cannot write

\-

I cannot think of origins
        they are too far back
               they are far too close

the world has forgotten us
        because there was nothing
            to remember

Melbourne
May – December 2001

Ah, sister! Desolation is a delicate thing.
—Shelley

multiple cloud layers
turbulence in the eye of
the calm
lifting off New Zealand soil—
tears and a simple distress
at the enormity and challenge
 of what I'm doing

-

it continues to astonish him that, at any moment, he expects to be
accosted 'by a perfect stranger', and made to account for his pretentious-
ness, his insincerity, his fraudulent behaviour, his flawed being

-

there is not enough time in a single life
for what we have written to become clear to us

-

at a painted parrot
on a shop window
two mynahs shout
their windy power

to share the footpath
purely with their kin
they preen and stoush
and kill the hour

-

the police wear guns
the rest wear mobile phones—
the world's your holster

-

Leonardo, again and again in old age—
Di mi se mai fu fatta alcuna cosa
Tell me if ever anything was finished

-

what is my life but the acting out of the body that gave me birth, my
mother. My father's role was punishment and abandonment—he had 'for-
saken me' before I was born. Oidipous was right to kill the bastard (who
of course, we are apt to forget, had tried to kill him! But my mother's
devastating plaint still rings in my ears—O, I did want you to make some-
thing of your life

-

how shall we live
in bright day's dark

without an irritable reaching
for the light

[*sine privilegio*]

-

words world
where 'world' is
a doing
word

-

in the distance, two whitish folded street umbrellas that looked, at first
glance, like tombstones

-

e-mailing Max this morning I mentioned the words 'spring to mind', as if,
even in this simplest and most everyday occurrence, all the talk, all over
the place, words, from the well-spring, the unsaid, the so-called uncon-
scious, *spring* to mind, that the old mystical 'leap of faith' (meaningless
to me, I am quoting) is exactly the process of everyone's talk, at any and
every level of conversation. Perhaps the issue is really that, instead of
fussing about where the words come from (from the shallows, from the
depths), whether the words, having sprung, leapt into the 'upper air' (the
air we breathe, simply that), they reach anything that can be legitimately
characterised as 'mind'. For talk, all of it, is creation out of nothing, crea-
tion out of everything

-

he is ever caught
in talk

in chatter's noose
you'll perish soon

breath's dearth
breaks the thread

only once you'll write
and tire

then I'd
die

-

for a moment, the traffic noise
almost stopped

-

it is still of interest to me that I am double, the lyricist and the technician. In the one, I cry out in pain and loss. In the other I resist, as far as I am able, any such reference, setting out the words as ruins of a world that nourishes no one. "To join the halves" I once wrote. If that can only happen at death (how that couple over there, in their eighties at a guess, carry their deaths with them with such dignity) and, if I am thus already dead, are the halves then already joined? It is we who fragment the world with words, with our appalling and magnificent desire to speak of this first, then that

-

it's terrible to have to say it, but supplanting one inscription for another is merely the normal state of affairs

-

the sea here, out on the pier at the end of Kerferd Street, is without sound. Not waves, but a rhythm of swells. Looking down, all thought can drown here, until a single light brown leaf, floating gently against the flow of waves, registers a kind of distance, a measure, before it moves out of vision beneath the pier, and the unfathomable deep (one or two fathoms, perhaps) wells from within you once more.

It is usually possible to give word to the breaking wave, the qualities of foam, the roar or splash of the outer edge of the meeting place of land and sea. But the scope of that meeting is the sea-floor itself, the expanse of earth under water upon which we cannot walk, where the oceans slosh about between their continental sides—however unlike bowl or cup those shifting boundaries are, however contrary their movement is as the waves come in while the tide goes out.

But this quiet, that wells in the heart as in the sea, in barely perceptual movement and no sound, is without resolution or content, unless content is the contentment felt if one is at rest. I am less and less persuaded that the 'human' heart is specifically 'human' after all. Unlike the cormorant flying out low over water we are without wings. But the words are winged. They travel in air as we cannot, and the imagination too is winged, for it can take us anywhere a bird can go as we remain rooted to the spot on which we stand. If the gull's cry is mine, if the sea swell is mine, if the dark grey naval ship in the bay is the darkness of our murderous interest in each other, then the heart is within us only by virtue (and never by virtue alone—"grace and disgrace" said William Saroyan— of the earth, the earth itself from which we have emerged over millennia, and which itself is at the core of the human heart

-

we have this arrangement
with words

they will arrange us
in their order

-

I am sick of words   sick of having to go to them
always, in my distress

-

I am living, house-minding for a few days, in a dwelling owned by a successful middle-class family, in which there is not one thing, no picture, no piece of furniture, plate, glass, cup or vase that I would choose for my own use

-

a swarm of tiny flies in the evening sunlight: they move at such speed it's a wonder they are not in continual collision with each other

-

Michelle Anderson: "the type in this book's too big for words"

-

his walk is a bit lanky, loose about the shoulders, with a perceptible sway or swing about it. She is upright, brisk and business-like, a crisp quick body alongside his

-

deep green leaf / light orange berries
little velvety leaf / dark red berries

-

the near-bare trunk of a gum tree—
charred suppurating flesh

-

the paperbark: as if, engorged with sap
the tree-skin splits into layer upon layer
of folded flapping pages
of an unreadable book

-

I wonder to what extent my 'observations of nature'
are possible because I don't know the names of things.
Is there something about the state of my ignorance
that makes much of my writing possible?

-

solitude
celibacy
poverty

-

a small elderly man, hands in trouser pockets, high-stepping across the
road, as if he is delicately avoiding contact with something we cannot see,
or as if he were doing exercises he hadn't done before leaving home

-

facing pages only face to face
in a closed book

-

rhapsode = stitcher

-

on the Yarra—three boats, each
in each other's wake

-

not happy with *Open leaves* as book title now. *Megaphonos* would give the game away, but the word Giorgio Agamben uses, which seems to be a kind of introduction or preface to a poem—'razo'—might work. I'm noticing too that I'm using non-English language words for titles: *Fragmenta nova, Megaphonos, Katalogos, Razo* etc. *Razo* has this nicety, that it suggests the poems themselves are introductory gestures towards works yet to appear—in the Book, but not in the book

-

re: Blanchot: the *disappointment* he notes concerning the fragment (he is writing in fragments!). But it is precisely its appointment I'm attracted to—the fragmented appointments I make with writing

-

with a quick warmth, of eyes and gesture, he reached out and put an ice-cold hand on the stranger's arm

-

eye of the crow—a ring of very light blue
red-eyed magpie

-

a woman, who refuses to wear make-up in public, but prepares her face with great care and precision before making love

-

seeing his image in a shop window, he is appalled that such a creature should exist

-

if only he were completely mad
perhaps he could live his life after all

-

one does not choose words
they simply flow out of one

-

what is to become of the 'my'
in 'my writing'

January – July 2002

Adumbrate nature. Walk a given path.
—Robert Creeley

"So you're writing yourself a novel are you Alan?"

(real estate agent viewing the house

-

"... an incoherence of inarticulate cries" (Mallarmé

but what of "...an incoherence of articulate cries"?
much more interesting

-

turning off the halogen lamp I like
the delay to full darkness
while the glow of the cooling bulb recedes

-

all's it
and it's
not all

-

at the Merri Creek—dragonfly ten to fifteen feet above water, flying down-
stream for ten to thirty feet then turning sharply back to almost where it
started, to do it again. How fast they turn, change direction, or even stay
in direction but shift suddenly sideways or alter elevation

-

rippling reflected light
on the underside of
overhanging branches
at water's edge

-

incredibly varied speed of
wing-flap, creature
to creature

-

gather all the books you want
the Book will elude you

-

signs of aging : moles and small red pimple-like structures on the skin,
slack breasts (mine), and slack muscles, veins showing on the feet

-

at the Northcote Mall—extraordinary levels of obesity—men and women
my age with huge stomachs unable to sit upright, but lean back as if they
are about to slide off the seat. Watching them getting in and out of their
cars is excruciating

-

random patterned
turns of swallows
over the pond

-

for a long time now I have wanted, at times desperately, to begin again.
It's impossible of course. But some kind of nostalgia for a beginning, a
new beginning, as if I could clear the mind and start all over. As if the
past was no more than a weight, not the accumulations of past experi-
ences, thoughts, feelings, events etc, but simply a weight, a great stone
slab on the back or shoulders one might simply throw off in a single shrug

-

'What thou seest, write in a book, and send it. . .' (*Revelations* of John

'There is no redemption on the page.' (Alberto Mengel

-

Larry Eigner   *birds keep*
                                          going out
                                                      of my mind

-

swallows dive to the surface
ducks below it

-

sparrows
& everything else
on the line

-

old man fastidiously rolls his trouser legs above the knees, walks to the
sea-edge, bends and rolls the left leg a little higher, wades into the shal-
lows, turns both trouser legs further up, curves his body down and scoops
with both hands the salt-water to his face very rapidly again and again for
some two to three minutes, then stands and turns to shore, at which point
I realise this person is a woman

-

giving thanks for/to something/someone
that/who does not care a damn for you

-

the Book as a haunting
        hunts you down
                escapes you

-

perhaps negotiating one's relation to the tradition is not about choosing
which bits to align with and which not, but how to move about the terri-
tory in all its multifariousness & unease without being destroyed by it. I
don't say, however, that it's easy to do, or that I succeed in it particularly

-

small orange moth or butterfly
fluttering up
the yellow-clay bank

-

suddenly, round the pond
all the birds begin grooming, flat out
as if late for something

-

a person in their twenties on the tram, with wide face, high cheekbones, full soft lips with slight downturn at their corners. When the head is turned in one direction it seemed definitely female, in the other direction definitely male

-

is the 'examined life' really worth living? My own, examined and found seriously wanting by a succession of relationships, would seem, by these judgments, not. When my own reflections find me deficient and dysfunctional—what's worth it in that? It strikes me an unreflective, unexamined life is greatly to be desired. . .

-

grey-bearded man, mid-sixties, waiting for a tram, takes from his pocket a little pair of scissors which he unfolds and begins clipping the beard around the corners of his mouth. As the traffic hurtles all around us he checks his progress with his tongue, going from one side of his mouth to the other, clipping again, checking with his tongue again, then folding up the scissors and pocketing them as the tram arrives

-

the pleasure of 'looking' thru the eyes of another who really did look. I'm
thinking of Joseph Joubert on rain, 1783

-

as if all he had to do was turn to her
and she'd turn to him

swallows over pond
dark above
light below

parrots over field
green above
red below

-

the technique in *Anne of the Iron Door*, where the research is never contra-
dicted but the gaps between the evidence are filled with pure invention,
could be applied to an autobiography—get the 'facts' into a time-line,
then tell a completely fictitious story which nonetheless includes all the
'facts' in their sequence

-

"you have to eat these
with yr legs open" she sd

-

between the pen-point
& its shadow
the words

in the lift-off
a small arc across
the light

light after light
the dark angel
eludes and
follows you

-

words: an excess per se
while the present is already
full to a brim that will
never overflow

or overflow is itself
the normal condition

the world does not ask for them
does not resist them
does not welcome them

is it that the human body *is*
other-worldly: that we

are aliens here
and out of place
in any place

-

the vomit of pure poetry

-

re-membering orpheus
dis-membered by maenids
by bassarids / the thracian women

torn apart / exile
from self & others

the thracian women / the muses
bury his head / the head
become oracle

to say this you have to die

-

green trees
blue sky

and they say
such colours
do not go
together

August – December 2002

Not enough and too much.
Herakleitos / Guy Davenport

André du Bouchet : "I write as far away from myself
as possible"

and Joubert again: "luminous words, like those drops of light
we see in fireworks"

-

he cannot make poems out of leaves, raindrops or tufts of cloud —

but from leaves
raindrops
tufts of cloud

he makes his move

-

letting go = learning to die

-

how good to abandon all sense of a 'literary career', in the name of
writing. Imperative at most times to refuse the 'blandishments' of suc-
cess. Imperative at times to acknowledge the community one is part of,
inevitably

-

as if mind shrunk
while body
bloated

he has yet to learn
to sit quietly

-

I would like my life to be over, so something else could begin.
Begging to begin, to begin being again.
                          (begging acknowledges
the depth to which we already depend upon others for *all*
our needs (Einstein allowing how much he receives from others,
wishing to *exert* himself to give in like measure

-

(Darebin Creek)   big tree, leafless, possibly dead, at water-edge,
half its twiggy branches covered in yellow/orange fungus or lichen

at several rocky points along the stream
patches of water flicking sunlight off the surface

-

am suddenly transfixed by sight of a white bird, size of a turtle-dove, on
the tip of the highest branch of a leafless tree, other side of the stream.
Dark patches on wing, dark beak, wondering if it was (thinking of bird pic-
tures I've seen) a white peregrine. It's looking down from some 10 metres
up on the slightly grey murky water of the creek. When it flies off I may
know more about it, its wing-tip, if it moves like a hawk, etc, but now
perched on such a small tip of a branch—not much of a hold on the world,
but enough. Swallows dart around it. Quick cry of another bird turns its
attention. Three ducks in the water, two crows overhead. Against a blue

sky with long white canoe-shaped cirrus just above. When it stretches a light grey wing out from time to time it lengthens its leg on the same side also. Short dark beak, forming a V-shape with its eyes. I waited for about twenty minutes to see it fly away, but it was still there when I decided to move on

-

at night, I like to know it's night, which is why I use low lamps & few of them. Under the desk lamp, ink from this pen shines while wet & reflects many colours, like spectra, until it dries & blackens

-

'Art hovers in the unsolved riddle'. —Karen Burns on Pat Brassington

-

'a book in the hand' is almost a tautology. For a book is a 'book' only when it is in the hands, is it not. One of the (sometimes written, sometimes not) signs on/of a painting is DO NOT TOUCH. But to 'know' about a particular volume is impossible without it being (its being) in the hands. To experience a painting you keep a (your) distance. To experience a book you touch it, and often, as you turn the pages. To some extent a painting acquires its status by the very prohibition to touch, a prohibition which is signified by distance. Opening a book demands an intimate proximity. Writing this notebook, it is on my knees—but if *I* were 'on my knees', something very different would be happening. . .

-

Tina rang from Brisbane last night : the sky, she sd, is higher there

She told me also about the birds around her house. Calls them 'blues birds', that they sang perfect blues phrases, and then she whistled them to me on the phone

-

Bruno showed me a lovely book he'd been given—paintings by Brice Marden—the book housed in a *magnetic chemise!*

-

where are you if in exile
in yr 'own' country

what's the difference
if any, between exile
& 'personal' alienation

-

out to Darebin Creek. Didn't write anything there, but saw two 'new' birds. One like a pigeon with a whitish cap on its forehead, a smudged rust under wing, dark markings on lower back. Other was a tiny bird with dark red flashes from beak, past the eyes almost to the back of the head, and the same red along the sides of its tail. Rest of bird a soft greeny fawn. Later sat on a wooden seat above stream and distant by about 100 metres, at edge of a small field of tall grass, some a metre high, ripening ears at tips. Lovely soft 'sea' of grass

-

Anne Hollander: ". . .in these portraits, you do not see the woman, you see the painting. This is the painter's business, and it is never not so". Interview with Julie Copeland

-

these men totally relaxed with their children—how far away from my experience

-

the pun: how insistent it has been for me. What is the pun but a joining of disparate parts, a real 'hesitation between sound & sense' (Valery). A connecting device

-

what I mean   by that
by that, he sd   I mean
is this   this

-

this morning found a red mole under my left arm

-

Agamben's notion that mannerism is psychiatrically improper: 'impropriety as not being one's self'. Talking with Caroline recently I was trying to understand why my work often offended people (in NZ). As if it were improper, or the term I used, bad-mannered. From Agamben's notes, it is the manneredness of the work that is at issue. Abandoning (it seems) one's personal style, the poet's voice, the authentic anthropological squawk, my experiments are experiments in *manner*, and *thereby* bad-mannered, improper

-

what is the gift to be renounced
whether one has fallen into things
or not fallen into things
                              (after reading the *Diamond Sutra*

-

for G.H.   I find my self
                             when all is lost

                             I find the world
                             when I am lost

December 2002 – July 2003

but me you have forgotten
Sappho / Anne Carson

he was (is) a nice man, and a bright one but, without any justification, I found his effusive self-confidence and naturally-worn success intimidating. For the rest of the day I did not shake off the feeling that I had let myself down in the conversation. I wonder if I will ever feel differently in these situations

-

what are tears for
unless they flow

-

at last, I have a desk, and can spread out my dictionaries. I haven't had this luxury for a long time

-

from D T Suzuki : "... the peace of poverty (for peace is only possible in poverty) is obtained after a fierce battle with the entire strength of your personality...the battle must rage in its full vigour and masculinity...Zen is quite emphatic about this".

-

to the great affirmative Yes!
say No!

to the great negative No!
say Yes!

for the rest—
put things down
pick things up

-

3am : hard to say what dread is. Waking, or coming to the end of the day, it seems to have no object, no thing that triggers it, nothing one is frightened of. Indeed, the 'of' seems inoperable here. Being alone for long periods, and still often for days without face to face conversation, is no doubt part of it. Solitude / isolation

-

I am back to some sort of beginning in reading ancient Chinese & Japanese poetry, and two great books found at the Uni Library here: *Sun at Midnight* by Muso Soseki, trans W S Merwin & Soiku Shigematsu (North Point Press 1989), [this poet contemporary with Dante, & born 1275], and *The Essential Basho* trans Sam Hamill [Basho born 1644, dies 1694], Shambala 1999. The English of both books is exquisite, and like a deep stream whose utterly clear waters disguise everything. Limpid language – o yes, I recall here Elizabeth Wilson's wonderful phrase, 'oasis of language'. I have become aware of just how powerful was the impact upon my very earliest writing of the translations of Chinese poetry by Arthur Waley especially of Han Shan – 'astonished, I find two tear-drops hang'. I want that almost clunky literalness, and the deep feeling that informs and enlivens it

-

Carmen Blacker on the Manyo Shu: '. . .in these short songs many words are like shot silk. They flash red or green or even blue as we move. The same sound refracts into two, three or several meanings, so that the poem reaches out further than the shortness of its span might imply. . .an inner core surrounded by unspoken yet powerful circles of images'

-

hot wind drives dead
leaves & newspaper pages
along the road

what journeyings!

at the end
I will know nothing more
than they will

-

having cut myself off from the seductions of the culture/society
it is very enjoyable being in the middle of them in Melbourne Central

-

passing a line of paperbarks
in Clarendon Street
one of them has an unusually
regular splay of 'pages', its bark
peeling in the normal layers

but once alongside, someone had
placed a newspaper deftly
in one of its branches—
newspaperbark

-

return, but not to 'roots' (the species long since pulled out of the ground), but beginnings. Mine are, believe it or not (Ripley will tell you), ancient Chinese & Japanese poetry (esp. Arthur Waley), Edward Conze on the Diamond & Heart Sutras, Sappho, Archilochos and the pre-Socratics. Loved Latin at school. And music-making, left behind so long ago. . .

-

a few days back I burned my hand & now have a large coin-sized wound. This morning I burned another finger on the toaster. I am being burned. In what respect, then, am I playing with fire

-

this job is hard to do
with so little to do

-

if I stand helpless
in my comfortable apartment
not knowing what
is to happen next

where, within me, can
I be at home

-

3 foxes   music   language
                                         t'ai chi

reward = the yellow arrow   song   words
                                           dance
the right & sufficient
means or weapons
of deliverance
& power   yellow arrow = the straight course
                             direct rays of the sun
                    unrefracted light

-

'every now & then
a tree speaks to me'
she sd, arms outstretched
in a small graveyard

-

the sadness of a woman who announces to a table at which five men sit,
that she wants to have sex with all of them, and not one responds to her

-

I may be an aging fox
he sd, but I'm still
a fox

-

he has printed out the Heart Sutra, its text beautifully presented, in Chinese. He cannot of course read it. Profundity on profundity, mosquito on mosquito

-

most nights he has the same almost unnerving experience—someone in the upstairs flat urinates at the same time he does

-

the preparatory measures are innumerable and endless—

nothing whatever
gets completed

-

note in *Unfettered Mind* : 'the principle in dying is to recognise
why, and in what way,
one should die'

-

sword   japanese   samurai   [t'ai chi
                object of ceremony
                object of victory
        found within the Yamata no Orichi - 'a dragonlike
serpent killed by the god of storms'

-

the great master
in front of you

is the obverse of
the great demon
behind you

defeat both

-

if I cannot find you
in the swirl of matter

at least I know
you are there

fire & steam hissing
out of you

-

let me hear you
sing
          with the words I have stolen
from you

-

upstairs
a woman's regular gasped-out
half-moans half-cries
for several minutes

then one last long drawn
diminuendo

-

I want a plain statement
that tells you nothing
plainly

-

morning sunlight in trees
leaves lit from within

-

to catch the one word that will always escape you

-

birdsong—hearing the unmediated other

-

what a heap of
nothing much
we become

we are estranged from whom
we are most familiar

\-

being a master has no implications about mastery

from 'master' to 'mastery' is less a derivation than
an assumption. Philology is not enough, sure
but don't leave home without it

\-

the forest's great early morning shout

so why aren't I or we out there
squawking whistling screeching cawing
the heart out

\-

Anne Carson: 'There is too much self in my writing'

\-

tiny birds with red flashes
over eyes, along tails, have no
interest in my enquiries
about their welfare. You sd 'shared

experiences', like the quiet walk
on a bridge, sunlight flickering
on water, talk of healing, of gathering
ephemeral lives into a clearing
not to be made visible. This
is what I was here for
to begin with

-

sitting alone
hour upon hour
what kind of life is it

in the slow uncurling
of a buried thought
attempting speech

-

even this eye
flushed with blood
after a drinking bout

can see the bronze
silver & gold moths
dead
at the door

-

your eyes tell me
everything I want to know
everything I don't

-

Max's *Zen* 1996 — the spectacle, one glass of a pair
     the thing you see
     the thing you see with
one-sided
one-eyed   eye-patch   piracy   dead-eye dick!

to see the heavens thru a telescope is to look thru one eye
monocular

-

Rene Char : 'Ta fascinate lingerie'
           'your fascinating lingerie'
                         He says so,
but he's speechless of its particulars, silent of its effects,
mute on the role it plays in his loving—which says a lot

-

the trouble with autumn
and being adept at landing
on one's feet, is that the leaves
keep falling, and I have had
to keep on landing

-

what's the point of
reading poetry on the train

a man suddenly calls
out 'Hey hey! My my!
Hey hey! My my!'

-

we say we have a secret
life, but you can't hide anything
in this town

-

half moon at midday
oak leaves rain down
in merest wind

-

the mild incongruity
of a chinese girl
in a tartan skirt

-

if the finest needle
went down thru fontanelle
travelled thru cortex, bridged
the halves, opened
channels for long-past sifted
memories, what stories
would old cells & selves
unravel

-

two rivers run thru me
lethe's balm of forgetfulness

& the other's clear sharp taste of
remembering

joined as caduceus
from which none
escapes

-

skin-folds increase
limbs take longer
to move these mornings

night's half-light
surrounds you
as arms legs body
around me

the trite words
in all their depth
pour out

'I love you'

ever & ever
again

-

I do not have enough
names for what I have seen
or see or who I have seen
or see

-

in the beginning was
no word there was no
word in the beginning
was no word

if anything was pure
it was the stones
before we talked
about them

-

it has been a perfect day
the sun, wind, birds & flowers
a good friend & much-needed rain
have each visited me
yet all day
I have longed for you

-

grey pigeons
flickering light
and dark turn
above this inter-
section of
people & things
circling over all

meeting places
each greeting
itself over
in a flash

-

you are always
on my mind
if you don't like it
why not give me
another thought

-

as if he were slow glass
the light taking forever
to pass thru him, caught
in mirrored refractions
inside the skin, as if
it went in thru the eye
never to get out again

-

there are times when what I envy most about Sappho are the holes in the papyrus. That so much can be, no, it's not 'left out' (tho John Wieners, sd Bob Creeley to me once, wanted to know how much of an experience can be left out and still have the language active), but just not there. All we 'know' is that something, of which we never know anything, is absent. Yet these little bits of words, isolated, spring like singular flares dotted about the void (the empty pages not to be borne), are my ordeal by fire, that I should face and feel so much from so little in these fiery syllables that I too would fling at anyone looking here. O yes, I envy her alright. At the edges of absence—depend upon it, 'it's all there'

-

if you think
in these words that address you
that you or anything of you
is to be found here
you are mistaken

-

it's full moon and you
are out of town

across the room a young woman sings
of a life of sorrow

all my materials fail me
when I think of you

how long will death
let us have together

-

word has come that Joanna Paul has died, found 'face down' in a hot pool
(the pool known as 'The Priest's Pool'). Ian Wedde told me years ago she
was colour-blind, one of the reasons her paintings were of such interest to
him. Her note to me—'keep it simple'—when I began *A brief description of
the whole world*. I am re-reading her *Unwrapping the body* and *Imogen*

-

on the train: looking up from time to time the disposition of passengers
changes, and so thereby does the very feel of what it is like to be there

-

those who are shell-shocked
by fact of being alive

-

I hate to say it, but the graffiti
is prettier than the flower garden

-

not sure if I've noted this before, but others' notions of how to scan a line
of verse continue to strike me as odd. How Babette Deutsch gets -˘ / -
for 'Earth receive', I don't know, for to do it, she breaks a word, and what
for? Should it not be -/ ˘- ? Her feet require 'Earthre ceive' I would have
thought. Nevertheless I would not belittle the much I have otherwise
learned from Ms Deutsch

-

PATIENT INFORMATION

New York London

11 November – 7 December 2003

a kind of leaving
when you arrive
Susan Stewart

a maze of interconnected or crossed straight & dotted lines marking off
areas for specific purposes - black, white, yellow, red

White & yellow van with sign on roof : FOLLOW ME

-

CLOSED WORK
IN PROGRESS

-

green fields
purple hills

-

after the edge of white cumulus—
sea the same blue
as sky

-

this bright blue of the sea—
we know that down there
it will be green

-

31,000 feet, no one lives
here, a perfect metaphor

for what's on the ground. Most
are asleep in front of screens
flashing anything but the round
earth waiting for them to die.
Two layers of cloud below
move in apparently opposite
directions, each thickening.
We are the sole vestiges of
a people that tears its limbs
off every day

-

night flying, two stars
out window, one left
one right, could they be
the morning star
the evening star

enjoying the impossible
ghosts of cumulus skidding
over dark land forms, peninsulas
jutting into the sea, then realise
slowly those far reaches
are the plane's wing

-

the window that gives you
the world in day's light
throws back yr reflected
face at night

-

1. I'm here, in a sense, not because I'm a poet, but because I've come to be known thru my published books. If there were no books, there'd be no basis for inviting me here.

2. Not only my books, I have printed & published the work of others. Printing implies typography. Morison's 'typography is the disposition of words upon the page' applies equally to poetry.

3. Traditional stanza forms are methodologies for ending the lines. If one's not using such forms, the question about just where one's lines stop and a fresh one begins becomes an issue.

4. When setting type by hand (one's own work and others') you learn how to read their work.

5. After my early mentor George South (early 1960s) my next teacher was Charles Olson, and it was Olson who showed me how the arrangements of words on the page cld act as a score for reading them.

6. Most readers and most editors (I'm thinking of the disastrous treatment of a Frank O'Hara poem in an English anthology) simply don't know how to read the carefully constructed spaces in the works of Olson, Duncan, Creeley, Levertov these days.

7. Most I think contemporary poets do not address the problem of line length and line space in the ways many poets used to, and as I still do for the most part.

8. I now write books and see everything I do as a writer as destined, not just for a book, but as a book. I see ahead the formal shaping possibilities for the poem in relation to the book it is already on the way to becoming.

9. 'Some want to be successful, but others want to be good.' But it's naive not to acknowledge that it's for books that any of us get known as something or something else.

10. *read 'Imago Mundi' and 'The Gifts'.*

-

early horizon
red dust
but the wing is pink

lipstick or polished nails
above wind-shear
cloud
         ice crystals
form slowly
on the window

-

Niagara Falls

dark green river
white & light green of the fall
double rainbow right
down to the water surface
mix of fierce energy
& repose

acres of rapids
edging the fall

beside the river
at the fall's top
the landing becomes
a flat ship moving
backwards

sudden saffron robes
even the buddha
carries a camera
brilliant orange
against the wall
of spray

at last—
on the other side of the world

a scattering of
tiny islands
before the fall

with morning, little
particles
of snow

-

train Buffalo/Depew to NYC

fields of leafless trees
striped with snow

2 & 3 storey houses
different shapes from
'ours', almost naked
in their exposure to
one another, no fences
trees or even gardens

-

across river a low hill, thru
the quick passing of trees,
is a large whale travelling
along with us

-

at Metropolitan Museum of Art saw half an El Greco show and all of a
Philip Guston (born Goldstein, which I did not know). Last night a din-
ner in honour of yrs truly by Max & Barbara, with print-out menu and
several guests. Max gets himself actively taught by others. I am always

the autodidact. It's clear I am very out of touch with my field if the field is poetry, while I am retrieving my printing field—shld do both. It strikes me this New York trip is the beginning of a whole new approach to the whole of what I do as poet & printer. It occurs to me also that I no longer have a thoughtful understanding of any poetry, including my own

-

for Max—here we are,
on the other side of the world

who's afraid of the big bad apple!

source / sun / seeing / nothing

even of a glass door
you won't know
what's on the other side

-

what do I learn from Max's books—
1. colour - it's bright
2. whole page as field
3. permission

-

Max's books an artist can draw/paint a cock, a cunt, breasts, mouths etc and they can be seen as drawing 'exercises'. But a writer can't write cock, cunt, breast, arse etc without appearing pornographic. Why couldn't a cock be as neutral a matter to write as a table, or the colour of a car

-

there is a door in this house which is a full, door-sized mirror. I undressed in front of it today and saw myself, this almost unrecognisable naked body, for the first time

-

wake up
         clean the body
                  dress it
                          forget it
get out of bed
         clear the space
                  prepare it for the day
                          forget it
step onto the floor
         swing, bend, turn, float
                  all the limbs, then
                          forget them

-

one does not want
symbols that are so specific
in their reference

or meaning that they are unable
to provoke a variety of
responses

-

I can visit NZ now

-

missing miriam

-

the words leach into
each other, but not
as colour does

a painter can use an image
repeatedly over a life—
can a poet do the same

is it that
the heart, the mind
wants, above & below
all else, mouth, cock, cunt
breast, to enrich
the heart, the mind

-

'he did it on his own violation'

-

on the plane above cloud
a circular rainbow with
the shadow-image of
the plane in its centre

-

trees beside the rail-tracks
flicking the late afternoon sun
on & off

-

back country road on the Cotswolds
3 small birds fly out
of a hedge in silence
1 twittering bird stays
in a tree

walking across fields
about 10 gates, each
with a different kind
of latch

-

at British Museum Standing Buddha, from Sarnath where he first taught, Gupta period c.435, right hand abhaya mudra, nothing to fear once taken refuge in Buddha teachings. Head protuberance, usnisa, superior wisdom, red/brown, about 4ft high - first Buddha image in front of which I pulsate. To look at it I had to stand on both feet

-

Herne Hill (next station after Brixton —there is history in this house, this family. Last night visited Carola, Nadia Lasserson's mother and widow of Miron Grindea, editor of ADAM magazine. She's 90 or 91, sharp as a tack and still looking after guests as charmingly as she is competent. "Oh, Miron, Miron, always Miron" she sd. But now in the Lasserson's back yard, sunny, slightly cool, traffic noise replacing bird noise as usual. Mike's son Ben has kindly given me a copy of ADAM 300 (!), dedicated to Jean Cocteau whose cover drawings were given to ADAM shortly before his death. Printed and part published by Curwen Press, this issue has material by Joyce, Chekhov, Maurois, H G Wells, Gorky, Koestler, Graves, Raine, Auden, Alvarez, Aragon, Wilde, Celan, Zadkine, Montale, Mansfield, Paz, Borges, Butor, Sexton, George MacBeth, Mankowitz, Roditi, Abse, Simenon, Milhaud, Peter Levi, Nathaniel Tarn, Bullock, and drawings by Modigliani, Chagall, Tzara, Proust etc etc etc

-

these very European Jews: music, literature, art and family are Everything. I have never known why this pattern rings such bells for me, there's nothing in my background to support it, but it does. There's something here I recognise, and at some deeper level than I am usually on

-

in my arms & out of them
my longing for you
does not cease

-

Turner at the Tate—how much more is gained by the late paintings by not being framed!
                    light / air / water / elemental energy
smallness of humans / tiny sail in impossible seas
          meeting places land & sea, people & elements, sea & cloud,
light & dark
                    and in so many works a small detail (house, person, animal, sail etc against a vast background (or ground

the late watercolour sketches, unfinished/unframed : great beauty

-

at Tate Modern—Donald Judd 1928-94 : *Untitled 1972*. copper, enamel & aluminium. Open box on floor approx 4 feet square and a metre high. People leaning over it, see it's 'empty' and immediately walk off. But inside, the reflections of the internal walls is a luscious red, as if the outer wall is a copper skin and the inner walls are red internal organs. The sharp external lines of the geometric box are, inside, bent, wavy, curvaceous almost, almost indeterminate in the occasional multiple reflections. Standing at the corners of the box gives a lovely lozenge. Hell? Luscious satin sheets? Dark & light everywhere within. Potentially endless mirrors standing square to the box. It is also a box in which nothing is to be placed. A denial of both functionality and non-functionality, because the box is already full to the very brim.

Sol Lewitt, b.1928. *The Location of Six Geometric Figures*, 1975. Beautiful proses beneath the figures. Etching on paper. At his *Five Open Geometric Structures* (1979, wood painted white) I see Leonardo.

One great room in which my whole being lifted—Styll, Rothko, Gottlieb, Gorky, Pollock, Kline, Krasner, Smith. Kline's *Meryon* 1960-61, like a bridge or clock tower (Charles Meryon, 19th C). Gorky *Waterfall* wonderfully suggestive, erotic, arms & legs of supine woman. The Rothko room: it seemed to me that instead of his rectangles being windows that let varying amounts of light in, they kept varying amounts of light out, and their edges genuine peripheral vision. Cy Twombly, *Quattro Stagioni* : Primavera, Estate, Autumno, Inverno (the pencil writings) full of light. Remember Brancusi's *Maias*tra, polished brass on stone. Degas: *Little Dancer Aged Fourteen* 1880-81 (one poor bloke entering the room spotted the Little Dancer, walked across quickly to it, and announced, *very* audibly, 'Ah! Cezanne!'

what I responded to clearly is artists of my generation. Later artists who crowd their surfaces with images from everywhere and of every kind do not interest me. Kiefer is too monumental for his own good (or at least for mine

-

at the V&A—a show on Gothic England across several centuries. I took a quick look at some of it and decided not to continue. Went instead to the Asia show and to Steiglitz photos of Georgia O'Keefe. But I was bothered by something about the Gothic show and went back to it. It is alien to me.

Its heavy christian symbolism and stolid British character all monoliterate and heavy-handed. It has no call in me, as if, in spite of my general British origins, this statuary, bowls, jugs, goblets, plates and pictures were all too weighty and elaborate. By contrast, the bowls, tea-bowls, vases & celadon ware of Korea, China & Japan were of much greater interest, were far more beautiful, were more of what I would like to live with than these English things. Give me Buddha instead of Christ any day&night

-

on Fast Train to Cambridge—too fast to read the railway station names

mist & rolling fields
crows in the air
quails on the ground

-

what a photograph permits is attentiveness to what is seen that actual presence would not permit. The photograph permits the gaze, invites it, is even, perhaps, a place where the gaze might have its fulfilment, its purest expression

-

Thailand—Barking at the Buddha
at Ubon Ratchanthani an elaborately carved temple, decorated with coloured glass as in a mosaic, colonnaded verandah all round beside a 2 or 3 storey timber-framed and corrugated iron shack that housed a bell. A saffron robed monk began, slowly, to strike the bell at day's close. A woman arrived on a motor scooter on the tank of which is a small black poodle, somewhat over-dressed, which excites the passions of a large number of local dogs (about 12 to 15) until the woman decides it's best to leave. The dogs then turned their attention to the ringing of the bell

and all take up positions around it and howl into the evening air until the monk ceases his work

-

awake 6.30am to sounds of sparrows, chickens, crickets and a micro-phoned voice reverberating about the house & grounds, the voice continuous like a wind floating & bouncing off surfaces. Turns out it's a radio broadcast to workers in the rice fields, keeping them up-to-date with local issues, politics etc

    raucous chooks
                          sparrows under eaves
            the broadcast is political
                geckos high on white walls
        bougainvilleas in dragon-pots
                white red orange grafted onto each other
        red & gold ribbons on plants
            padlocked gate to keep the neighbours out, those
                who just walk, not speaking,
            just looking around

    on the courtyard deck
        her clothes, outer & inner
            are hanging out to dry
the woods here are all hard
        nothing soft like pine, the big
            old trees are protected (sacred
and many plants are poisonous

my brother grows orchids
        many colours with many
            different ways of growing (some
on the trunks of trees, the roots
        hanging in air waiting for water,
            some in shade, some in full sun
and Miriam photographing everything

gecko watching, its head
     just up between deck and wall
        sparrows all over
butterflies, esp one soft dark green
         as if underlaid with orange, more
    a sense of colour than a sight of it
but on its lower wings a small patch of
    light blue at the edges

Mekong river restaurant, across water is Laos
      the water all moving lines—black, white,
          dun, blue, grey, silver and all
opaque
      and the long-tailed boats, likely
their engines are from trucks left
after the Vietnam war

    in a hammock in good shade
        large dry leaves clattering against
    each other, who am I
      where is my buddha nature
in this soft warm wind, there's a man with no hands
    and a false leg begging at the roadside
        the trees flower at different seasons
and fill the night air with fragrances

29.12.03